KIDS

Scrapbooking
Easy as 1·2·3

Designed by

Written by

Debby Schuh Julie Stephani

INTRODUCTION

Welcome to the fun hobby of Scrapbooking! You probably have great pictures of your family, friends, and yourself. There are many fun things you can do with your pictures to save them in a very special way. That's what Scrapbooking is all about! It is so much more than just putting your picture in a photo album. It is storing them in a safe place, using materials that won't harm your pictures, and creating wonderful ways to display your pictures to make them look even better. Someday your children (and grandchildren!) can look at your scrapbooks and know who you were and what things you did during your lifetime.

So what is Scrapbooking? It is displaying your pictures on creative pages in an album to tell the story about you. There is an old saying, "A picture is worth a thousand words." It's true! You don't have to write a lot of words to tell your story if you have pictures to help you.

Both authors used to be schoolteachers, and now they get to combine their love of teaching with their favorite hobby. Debby teaches Scrapbooking classes at her local Michaels Arts & Crafts store, and she designed all of the great album pages throughout the book. Julie teaches Scrapbooking on TV and in workshops across the country. She wrote the basic instructions, compiled, and edited the book. They will share lots of quick tips they've learned to make Scrapbooking easier and more fun for you.

You may want to make the pages look exactly like the ones in this book — but you can also enjoy looking at the ideas and then do it your own way. Have fun!

We celebrate your creativity!

krause publications
An F&W Publications Company

700 East State Street • Iola, WI 54990-0001
715-445-2214 • 888-457-2873
www.krause.com

Library of Congress Catalog Card Number: 2002107625

ISBN 0-87349-412-1
Manufactured in the United States of America

WHERE TO FIND IT

Basic Instructions

Getting Started 4
Supplies 5-9
Cropping Photos 10
Photo Frames 11
Planning A Page 12
Journaling 13
Protecting 13
Basic Slide 44

Page Ideas

Beach Bums 14
Sleepover Party 15
Summer Flies By 16
Trip Time 17
My Life Booklets 19-21
Say Cheese 22
You're a Star 23
Happy Birthday (stars) 25
Soccer Season 26
Wet 'n Wild 27
Cute As a Bug 28
My Friends 31
Growing By Leaps & Bounds 33
Happy Birthday (tags) 34
Faithful Friends 36
Disney Days 37
Back To Class 38
Mini Album 39
It's Pumpkin Time 41
Dear Santa 43
Sliding on Cherry Hill 45

Patterns

Sleepover Party 18
Trip Time 18
Circles 21
You're a Star 23
Say Cheese 23
Stars 24
Growing By Leaps & Bounds 24
Soccer Season 24
Cute As A Bug 29-30
Wet 'n Wild 30
Disney Days 32
Back To Class 35
It's Pumpkin Time 40
Hearts 42
Dear Santa 42
Sliding on Cherry Hill 42
Slide Platform 44

Glossary 46

Sources 47

GETTING STARTED
10 EASY STEPS

1 Collect & Organize Photos
Group photos together by each event.

2 Collect & Organize Supplies
Begin with basic tools and supplies that you probably have around the house.

3 Choose A Theme & Pick Photos
Decide which photos to use and arrange them on one or two pages, depending on how many you have.

4 Crop Photos
Decide which photos need trimming and which ones would look good cut into a shape. See page 10.

5 Frame Photos
Use paper to make frames around photos. See page 11.

6 Add Details
Decide what to add to your page such as a title, stickers, die-cuts (paper shapes), borders, etc.

7 Arrange Pieces on Page
Place everything on your page (or pages) and have fun moving things around until you find the way you like best. See page 12.

8 Glue Pieces on Page
When everything is in place on your page (or pages), glue them down.

9 Journal on Pages
Write down the facts or details about the photos and event. See page 13.

10 Protect Photos & Pages
Store unused photos in photo-safe containers in a dry place that is not too hot or cold. Place finished pages in protective plastic sleeves. Collect your pages in an album.

BASIC SUPPLIES

There are many scrapbooking supplies to choose from but begin with the basics. Add more tools and materials as you go.

Begin with the following supplies:

* Album
* Paper
* Scissors
* Adhesive
* Pen
* Pencil
* Marker
* Ruler
* Eraser

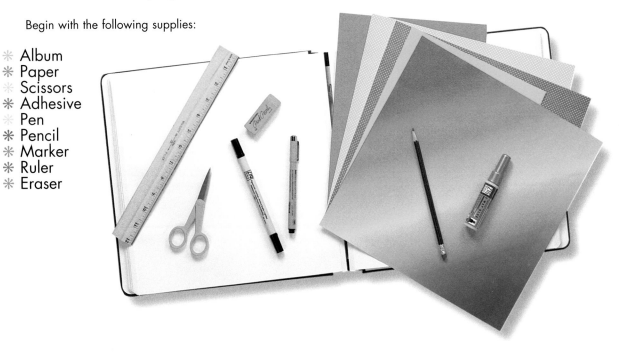

WHICH ALBUM?

Albums come in many different sizes. The smallest mini albums are only 3" x 3" which is just the right size for small class pictures of your friends.

The sizes of albums most often used are 8½" x 11" or 12" x 12". The size and style you choose depends on what you want to put into it.

Make sure you only use photo-safe materials in your albums and protect your pages with plastic protective sleeves.

ALBUM BINDINGS

The pages in albums are held together in different ways. The most common bindings are shown on this page. Read the description of each one to decide which type will be best for your scrapbooking project.

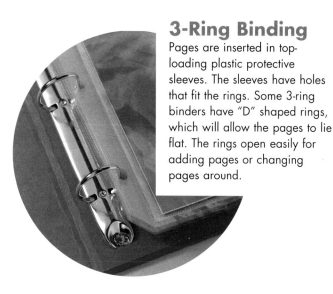

3-Ring Binding

Pages are inserted in top-loading plastic protective sleeves. The sleeves have holes that fit the rings. Some 3-ring binders have "D" shaped rings, which will allow the pages to lie flat. The rings open easily for adding pages or changing pages around.

Post Binding

Screws in the binding hold the album together. The screws can be removed so you can add pages or move them around. You can also add "extension" posts if you want to add extra pages.

Stitch Binding

The number of pages is fixed, so you can't add pages or change them around. They are good for special theme or gift albums.

Spiral Binding

Pages can not be added and pages can not be moved around. This album works well for one special subject or event – and also for gift albums. Sometimes they do not have protective plastic sleeves. Pages lie flat when open.

Strap Binding

Plastic straps are woven through strong staples that are attached to the pages. The protective sleeves can be removed while you work on the pages and then can be put back on. The pages lie flat and extra pages can be added.

Papers

MORE SUPPLIES . . .

Papers come in many different sizes, colors, and patterns. There are shiny metallic papers, and vellum is a semi-transparent paper.

Pens come in many photo-safe ink colors and have different size tips.

Markers also come in different colors and have different size tips that are even different shapes. Some markers have a different tip on each end.

Gel Pens have inks with bright colors and some are metallic with sparkles. Opaque ink shows up on dark paper — even on black.

Chalk adds soft color and can be used for shading.

Colored Pencils will also give you soft colors.

Rubber Stamps can be colored with ink, chalks, pencils, markers, or paints.

Pens

Markers

Gel Pens

Colored Pencils

Rubber Stamps

Chalk

Decorative-Edge Scissors

Straight-Edge Scissors

Punches

AND MORE SUPPLIES . . .

Scissors can be straight-edge or decorative-edge. They are used to cut creative paper frames, borders, and shapes. There are many decorative-edge patterns.

Punches come in many different styles that you can hold in your hand and squeeze —or press down on with your thumb or with the palm of your hand. They can punch large and small shapes of all kinds.

Knives should only be used if an adult is helping you. A craft knife is used to cut straight lines, and the swivel knife is used to cut around curves.

A **Cutting Mat** is used whenever you are cutting with a craft knife. It will protect your working surface and will allow the knife to cut smoothly.

A **Clear Ruler** will help you see where to place it better.

A **Paper Trimmer** is used to make a straight cut on paper. Paper is placed under the guide, and a blade runs down through the channel in the guide. Never touch the sharp blade and have an adult change the blade if it becomes dull.

Clear Ruler

Paper Trimmer

Craft Knife

Swivel Knife

Cutting Mat

Photo Corners

Foam Dots

Adhesives

Tracing Templates

Cutting Templates

Craft Knives

Die Cuts

Stickers

Adhesives should always be acid-free.

Photo Corners can be used to hold a photo in place by the corners. They can also be used just for decoration.

Dimensional Foam Dots have sticky tape on both sides with a layer of foam in between. They add dimension to items on the page.

Tracing Templates are used to trace shapes, letters, numbers, and borders.

Cutting Templates are used to cut shapes, letters, numbers, and borders. A craft knife is used in place of a pencil but always ask an adult for help before using one.

Die-Cuts come in hundreds of shapes and sizes. You can buy them already cut or they can be cut using a die-cutting machine.

Stickers are a quick way to add color to your pages.

CROPPING PHOTOS

Cropping a photo means that you cut away the unimportant background of a photo to make it a better one. NEVER cut a photo that is one-of-a-kind. Use a copy or reprint of the photo if you want to trim it. Most photos are best when they are not cropped too much.

BETTER

BEST

The doorframe and all of the clutter takes away from the subject of this photo.

The photo is better when it is cropped, but the background is still distracting.

The focus is on the girl and the bubble when the background is cut away completely.

See how different the same photo looks when it is cropped in different shapes.

Save fun shapes for fun photos! Use a plastic template to trace the shape on the photo and cut it out.

"Bumping" a photo is when you cut out around only part of a person or thing.

When you "silhouette" a person by cutting all around him (or her), be sure to leave a very thin border so the photo doesn't look too chopped.

PHOTO FRAMES

Photos often look better when they have colorful borders. Make your own frames easily by gluing the photo on paper and cutting around it, leaving a border. It is called "mounting" the photo. "Matting" a photo is making a frame and placing it over a photo.

Apply glue to back of the photo.

Press photo on paper.

Draw a line around the photo.

Cut along the line with a scissors.

Erase the pencil lines.

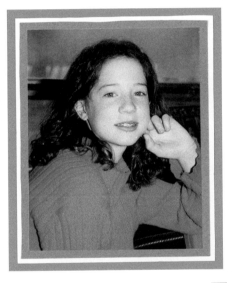

Repeat Steps 1 through 5 to make more than one border around the photo. Change the widths of the frames for a more interesting look.

Use straight and decorative-edge scissors.

Use both plain and pattern paper.

Make two frames the same size but in different colors. Tilt one of them behind the other.

Make a frame wide enough to add stickers and journaling. Cut around the stickers instead of making a frame with straight edges.

PLANNING A PAGE

The arrangement of photos, letters, shapes, and journaling on a page is called the layout. A good layout tells a story and organizes the page so the eye travels through the page easily. The upper left corner is usually looked at first and eyes naturally look from left to right. Experiment by moving pieces around on your page before gluing them down.

A Point of Interest

A page needs a main point of interest that the eye is drawn to first. You can draw attention to something in different ways. Make a photo larger, place it in the center of the page, or frame it in a special way with the brightest colors on the page.

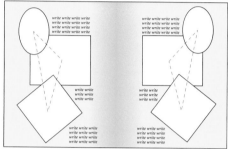

Symmetrical

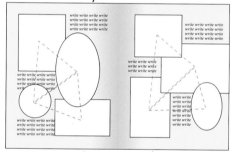

Asymmetrical

A Balanced Page

Items on the page have "weight." When two things weigh the same, they are balanced. They have more weight if they are larger, brighter in color, or have more details.

A page should have balance from left to right and from top to bottom. That doesn't mean two pages must be exactly the same (symmetrical). Pages that are not the same (asymmetrical) can be balanced, too. For example, one large photo can be balanced by two smaller ones.

Use the triangle pattern to arrange photos. When using more than three photos, you will have more than one triangle.

Variation

Use different sizes and shapes of photos to add interest to your pages.

Connecting Photos

Overlap items on the page to guide eyes as they travel from one to the next.

Color

Choose papers that bring out the colors in your photos. Use contrasting colors to separate one piece from another.

JOURNALING

Tell the story behind the photos in your albums. To get the basic facts, answer the following questions:
Who? What? When? Where? Why? How?

You can also make a pocket on the back of your page to hold additional information.

If all of the information doesn't fit on your page (like the names of everyone in a group photo or important details) make a pocket to hold the extra journaling.

A small booklet on your album page can hold more photos and journaling.

Collect, organize, and store photos and negatives in photo-safe boxes or albums.

PROTECTING

It is important to protect your photos and pages. Be aware of the things that are most harmful to them.

Photo Dangers

* Sunlight
* Humidity
* Felt-Tip Pen
* "Magnetic" Album
* Very Hot Temperatures
* Dust & Dirt
* Ball-Point Pen
* Fingerprints
* Acidity
* Very Cold Temperatures

Place finished pages in protective plastic sleeves.

BEACH BUMS

Use punches to make a "scene" at the beach!

WHAT YOU NEED

12" x 12" Paper:
- ❏ 1 tan sand*

12" x 12" Cardstock:
- ❏ 1 white
- ❏ 1 cream (background)
- ❏ 1 blue

8½" x 11" Cardstock:
- ❏ 1 red
- ❏ 1 blue

Scraps of Cardstock:
- ❏ yellow
- ❏ orange
- ❏ Large white tag*
- ❏ 10" of red yarn
- ❏ Red ¾" letter stickers

Punches*:
- ❏ small star
- ❏ fish
- ❏ sailboat
- ❏ crab
- ❏ sandcastle
- ❏ circles: ¼", ¾"

Fine-tip markers:
- ❏ yellow
- ❏ black
- ❏ Adhesive
- ❏ Paper trimmer
- ❏ Pencil
- ❏ Ruler
- ❏ Scissors

*These products were used: K & Co. paper • Paper Reflections tag • EK Success™ Paper Shapers® punches • Marvy® Uchida star punch

WHAT YOU DO

1 To tear paper, hold left side of the paper down on your work surface with left hand and pull the other side toward you with right hand. For sand, tear one 2" x 12" strip from tan paper. For water, tear one 3" x 12" strip and one 4" x 12" strip from blue cardstock. Overlap pieces as shown and glue down, leaving tops open to insert photos.

2 To decorate tag, tear one 1" x 6¼" strip from blue paper. Glue along bottom of tag. Tear one ½" x 6¼" strip from tan paper. Glue on top of blue paper. Turn card over and cut the blue and tan paper even with the edges of tag.

3 Glue tag on red cardstock. Cut around tag, leaving a thin border. Punch ¼" hole in red cardstock. **Option:** *To make your own tag, cut one white 3¼" x 6¼" piece of cardstock. Cut corners on one end at angles. Finish same as purchased tag.*

4 Punch out the following pieces: 2 orange fish, 2 red crabs, 1 blue sailboat, 2 tan sandcastles, 1 yellow ¾" circle (sun). Arrange punch shapes on the tag. Glue down. For title, press letter stickers on tag. Draw seagulls with black marker. Draw sun rays with yellow marker. Fold red yarn in half. Push loop end through hole in the tag. Slip two ends together through the loop and pull tightly.

5 For photo corners, cut one blue 1½" square and two red 1½" squares. Cut in half diagonally. Punch out six small stars from yellow cardstock. Glue one on each triangle.

6 Glue photos on red or blue cardstock. Cut around photos, leaving a thin border. Arrange pieces on page. Tuck two photos into the waves and sand. Glue down. Glue triangles on corners of photos as shown.

7 Add journaling across sand with black marker.

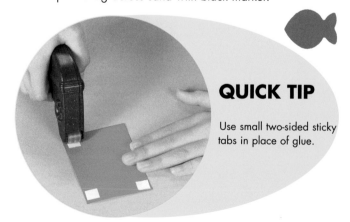

QUICK TIP

Use small two-sided sticky tabs in place of glue.

SLEEPOVER PARTY

Make a fun border along the bottom of the pages and use a flower punch to make the popcorn!

WHAT YOU NEED

12" x 12" Paper:
- ❏ 3 rainbow (background)
- ❏ 1 yellow embossed*

8½" x 11" Cardstock:
- ❏ 2 red

Scraps of Cardstock:
- ❏ yellow
- ❏ purple
- ❏ Black ½" letter stickers*

- ❏ Bedtime paper doll kit*
- ❏ 1" flower punch*
- ❏ Fine-tip black marker
- ❏ Adhesive
- ❏ Paper trimmer
- ❏ Pencil
- ❏ Ruler
- ❏ Scissors

Optional: Provo Craft® Coluzzle® cutting templates can be used for alphabet and circles. Making Memories die cuts can be used for popcorn box and phone.

*These products were used: Amscan paper • Making Memories paper, die cuts • Provo Craft® stickers • Coluzzle® cutting templates, knife, mat • EK Success™ Paperkin® paper doll kit • Marvy® Uchida punch

WHAT YOU DO

Trace and cut out red patterns on page 18 and #9 circle on page 21.

1 For border, cut two 3" x 12" strips from yellow paper. Cut two ½" x 12" strips from rainbow paper. Glue the rainbow strips on yellow strips. Glue one strip along bottom of each page.

2 To decorate border, glue paper doll pieces from kit together, making the paper doll, teddy bear, pillow, and book. With black marker, doodle lines and dots on each piece. Write "My Diary" on the front of the book. Trace and cut out phone from purple paper and popcorn box from red paper. Doodle lines and dots on telephone and popcorn box. For popcorn, punch out six flowers from yellow cardstock. Trace and cut out letters from red cardstock. **Option:** *Use red 2" letter stickers.*

3 Arrange pieces on pages. Press black letter stickers in place. Glue pieces down.

4 Glue three photos on yellow paper. Cut around photos, leaving a thin border. Trace circles on two photos and cut out. Glue all photos on red paper. Cut around photos, leaving a thin border. Arrange photos on pages. Glue down.

5 Add journaling with black marker.

SUMMER FLIES BY

Decorate die cuts with glitter and rhinestones to add a sparkle to your summer photos!

WHAT YOU NEED

12" x 12" Cardstock:
- ❑ 2 yellow (background)
- ❑ 1 purple

8½" x 11" Cardstock:
- ❑ 1 blue
- ❑ 1 purple

- ❑ Yellow 1" letter stickers*

Printed die cuts*:
- ❑ butterflies
- ❑ flowers

- ❑ Rhinestones
- ❑ Purple glitter
- ❑ Fine-tip black marker
- ❑ White glue
- ❑ Adhesive
- ❑ Paper trimmer
- ❑ Pencil
- ❑ Ruler
- ❑ Scissors
- ❑ Toothpick

*These products were used: Provo Craft® letter stickers • Wallies die cuts

WHAT YOU DO

1 To decorate the flowers, use a toothpick to cover the swirl in the center of the flower with a line of glue. Sprinkle glitter on glue. Shake off extra glitter. Set aside to dry.

2 To decorate butterflies, cover dots on the body or the whole body with glue. Sprinkle glitter on glue. Shake off extra glitter. For rhinestones, place dot of glue on the butterfly spots. Set rhinestone on the dot of glue. Set aside to dry.

3 For background, tear two 3" x 12" strips from purple cardstock. To tear paper, hold left side of the paper down on your work surface with left hand and pull the other side toward you with right hand. Glue along top of both pages. With black marker, doodle lines, dots, and dashes around purple and yellow cardstock.

4 Glue a butterfly on each end of the purple border strips. For title, press letter stickers across top of pages. To add rhinestones, place dot of glue on the purple strip. Set rhinestone on the dot of glue. To show motion, draw lines near butterflies and letters with a black marker as shown.

5 Glue photos on blue or purple cardstock. Cut around photos, leaving a thin border.

6 Arrange pieces on the pages. Glue down. With black marker, doodle dots around flowers.

7 Add journaling with black marker.

QUICK TIP

See the pink flower on these pages? To tie two pages together, cut a shape in half and glue one half on each page – right across from each other.

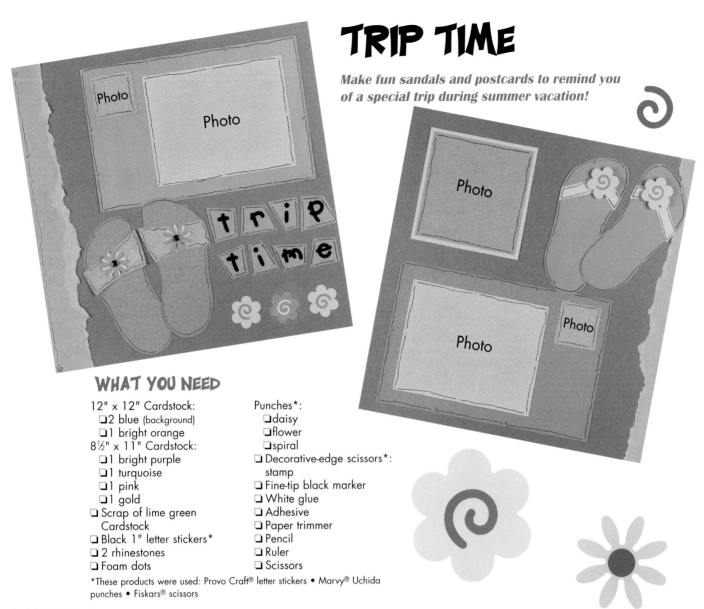

TRIP TIME

Make fun sandals and postcards to remind you of a special trip during summer vacation!

WHAT YOU NEED

12" x 12" Cardstock:
- ❏ 2 blue (background)
- ❏ 1 bright orange

8½" x 11" Cardstock:
- ❏ 1 bright purple
- ❏ 1 turquoise
- ❏ 1 pink
- ❏ 1 gold
- ❏ Scrap of lime green Cardstock
- ❏ Black 1" letter stickers*
- ❏ 2 rhinestones
- ❏ Foam dots

Punches*:
- ❏ daisy
- ❏ flower
- ❏ spiral
- ❏ Decorative-edge scissors*: stamp
- ❏ Fine-tip black marker
- ❏ White glue
- ❏ Adhesive
- ❏ Paper trimmer
- ❏ Pencil
- ❏ Ruler
- ❏ Scissors

*These products were used: Provo Craft® letter stickers • Marvy® Uchida punches • Fiskars® scissors

WHAT YOU DO

Trace and cut out blue patterns on page 18.

1 For borders, tear two 1½" x 12" strips from orange cardstock. To tear cardstock, place left hand on the paper on your work surface. Pull the right side of the paper toward you with right hand. Glue strips on blue background along the outside edge of each page.

2 Trace and cut out two purple and two turquoise sandals. For purple sandals, cut out two orange #1 straps and glue in place. Punch two gold and two turquoise daisies. Glue on straps. Place a drop of glue in the center of each daisy and press a rhinestone on the glue. For turquoise sandals, cut two gold #2 straps. Punch two lime green flowers and two purple spirals. Glue the spirals on the flowers. Peel paper off two foam dots and press one on back of each flower. Peel paper off other side of foam dots and press flowers on the straps. With black marker, doodle lines, dots, and dashes on sandals.

3 For title, press the letter "t" sticker on pink cardstock. Cut four straight sides around the letter at different angles. With black marker, doodle lines and dots along edges. Repeat steps for the other letters. Punch out two lime green and one purple flower. Punch two purple and one lime green spiral. Glue a spiral on the center of each flower.

4 For postcards, cut one 5½" x 8½" piece from turquoise paper, and one from purple paper. For stamps, cut two 2" orange squares. Cut around each side of the squares with the stamp-edge scissors. Cut two 1" square photos and glue on orange squares. Glue two photos on gold paper and one photo on pink paper. Trim paper around photos, leaving a thin border. Glue pink framed photo on gold paper. Trim paper again, leaving a thin gold border.

5 Arrange pieces on page. Glue down. Doodle lines, dots, and dashes along edges of each piece.

6 Add journaling with black marker.

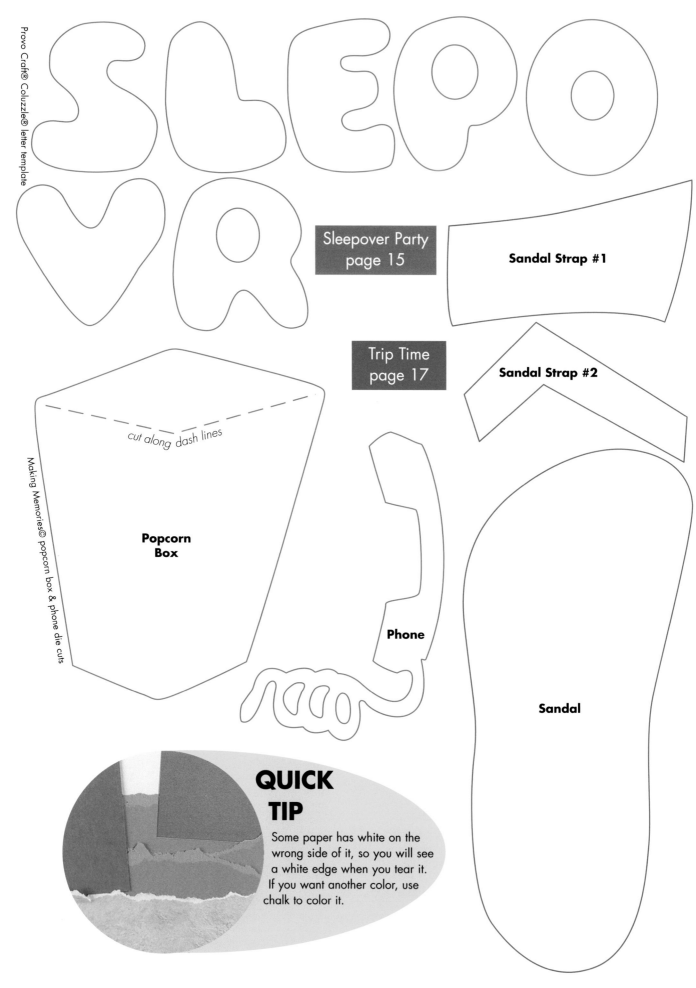

Provo Craft® Coluzzle® letter template

SLEPO VR

Sleepover Party
page 15

Sandal Strap #1

Trip Time
page 17

Sandal Strap #2

cut along dash lines

Making Memories© popcorn box & phone die cuts

Popcorn Box

Phone

Sandal

QUICK TIP

Some paper has white on the wrong side of it, so you will see a white edge when you tear it. If you want another color, use chalk to color it.

MY LIFE ACCORDING TO ME

Use colorful pattern papers to make a fun album all about you!

WHAT YOU NEED

- ❏ 5½" x 8½" 3-ring binder
- ❏ 5½" x 8½" 3-ring page protectors
- ❏ 8½" x 11" Paper: *Bright Great Backgrounds* book Cardstock:
  - ❏ 1 red
  - ❏ 1 blue
  - ❏ 1 green
  - ❏ 1 yellow
- ❏ Black ½" letter stickers*
- ❏ Boy paper doll kit*

- ❏ Die-cut kit: *Boy Theme*
- ❏ Die-cut words: mommy, daddy
- ❏ Decorative-edge scissors
- ❏ Fine-tip black marker
- ❏ Adhesive
- ❏ Paper trimmer
- ❏ Pencil
- ❏ Ruler
- ❏ Scissors

* These products were used: Hot Off the Press paper • Provo Craft® letter stickers • EK Success™ Paperkin® paper doll kit • ScrapEase die-cut kit • Making Memories die cuts

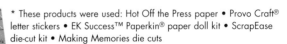

WHAT YOU DO

1 For background pages, cut pattern paper in half to measure 5½" x 8½". For cover, glue pieces of the paper doll kit together. For title, cut one 2¼" x 4" piece from green cardstock. Press letter stickers on green piece. Glue green piece on blue paper. Trim around title with decorative scissors, leaving a ½" border. Arrange pieces on background page. Glue down. Glue page on yellow paper. Trim around page, leaving a thin border. Glue on album cover.

2 For inside pages, use stickers and die cuts to decorate the pages. Suggested titles: My Picture, Mom (cutting off the "my"), Dad (cut off the "dy"), My Friends, My Travels, and Someday.

3 Add photos with paper frames and journaling.

The album can be made to fit anyone's special personality and interests.

MY LIFE ACCORDING TO ME

Make your own album journal! Use gel pens on black paper to decorate a fun book to hold your special photos and thoughts!

WHAT YOU NEED

8½" x 11" Cardstock:
- ❏ 5 black

Scraps of Cardstock:
- ❏ 1 lime green
- ❏ 1 pink
- ❏ 1 turquoise
- ❏ 1 yellow
- ❏ 1 white
- ❏ Birthday paper doll kit*
- ❏ Gel Roller accessory kit*
- ❏ Gel pens

Punches*:
- ❏ flower
- ❏ circle
- ❏ heart
- ❏ star
- ❏ Decorative-edge scissors*: cloud
- ❏ Fine-tip black marker
- ❏ Adhesive
- ❏ Paper trimmer
- ❏ Pencil
- ❏ Ruler
- ❏ Scissors

Optional: One black ⅜" plastic binding comb* or 18" of yarn or ¼" ribbon

*These products were used: EK Success™ Paperkin® paper doll kit
• Amscan Memory Kit accessory kit • Marvy® Uchida punches
• Fiskars® scissors • ibico binding comb

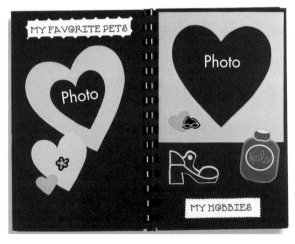

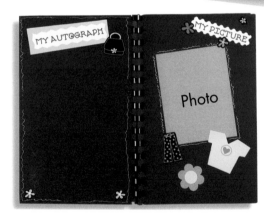

WHAT YOU DO

1 For book pages, cut 5½" x 8½" pieces from black cardstock. For binding, check at your local office supply store for a comb-binding machine. It can be used to punch the holes in all pages. Use the machine to insert the binding or slide the binding through the holes one at a time. **Options:** *Punch three holes along one side of each page with a hole punch. Tie the pages together with yarn or ribbon. Pages can also be stapled together.*

2 For book cover, glue pieces of the paper doll kit together. With black marker, print the title on white cardstock. **Options:** *Type the title on a computer and print it on white*

cardstock or use stickers to make the title. Cut around the title with the cloud-edge scissors. Glue on lime green paper. Cut around title, leaving a thin border. Arrange pieces on page. Glue down.

3 For inside pages of the book, decorate the pages with stickers, frames, and die cuts. Add punches. Print titles on the pages. Frame photos with paper. With gel pens, doodle lines, dots, and swirls on the pages.

4 Add journaling and photos.

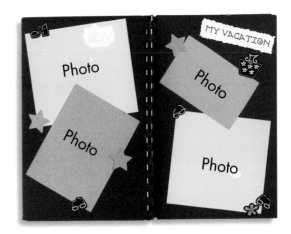

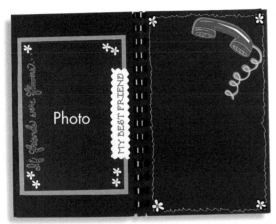

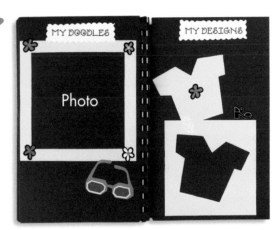

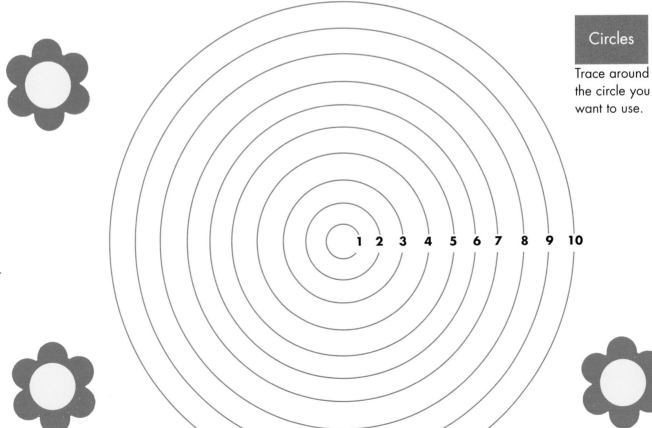

Circles

Trace around the circle you want to use.

SAY CHEESE

Use a hole punch to make these fun frames.
Someone has been snacking!

WHAT YOU NEED

12" x 12" Cardstock:
- ❑ 1 black

12"x12" Yellow paper*:
- ❑ 1 print (background)
- ❑ 1 dot
- ❑ 1 check

8½" x 11" Cardstock:
- ❑ 2 yellow

Scraps of Cardstock:
- ❑ gray
- ❑ pink
- ❑ 10" of ⅜" black polka-dot ribbon*

- ❑ Yellow 1" letter stickers*

Punches*:
- ❑ circle - ¼" , ½"
- ❑ spiral - ½", 1"
- ❑ White gel pen
- ❑ Fine-tip black marker
- ❑ Adhesive
- ❑ Paper trimmer
- ❑ Pencil
- ❑ Ruler
- ❑ Scissors

*These products were used: Provo Craft® papers, letter stickers • Offray ribbon • Marvy® Uchida punches

Make a small booklet to hold more photos!

WHAT YOU DO

Trace and cut out red patterns on page 23.

1 For mice, trace and cut out one large and one small body from gray cardstock. Punch out the following pieces from cardstock:
Gray - two ½" circles, one ½" spiral, one 1" spiral
Pink - two ¼" circles
Black - two ¼" circles
Glue mice together as shown. Draw eyes with black marker.

2 Cut one 4¼" x 6" piece from yellow paper. Cut out inside of rectangle, leaving a ½" frame. Punch ¼" holes here and there in the frame. Cut one 4¾" x 6½" piece from black paper. Glue frame on the black mat. Cut photo to fit inside frame. Glue down.

3 For border, cut one 2¼" x 11" strip from black paper. Cut one 1" x 11" strip from yellow paper. Tear paper along one long edge. Glue black strip over straight edge of yellow strip. Press letters and large mouse on border as shown. With white gel pen, doodle three dots three times.

4 To make the booklet, cut one 7¼" x 9½" cover piece from yellow dot paper. Fold in half. For inside pages, cut four 6¾" x 9" pieces from other yellow print papers. Fold pages in half. Glue pages together along folds. Glue the wrong side of the first page to the inside of the front cover. Glue the wrong side of the last page to the inside of the back cover. Cut photos to fit and glue inside. Journal in the booklet with black marker.

5 For booklet cover, cut one 3" x 5" piece from black paper. Glue on yellow paper. Cut around rectangle, leaving a thin border. Punch two holes in top center of rectangle. Insert ends of ribbon through holes from front to back. Insert ends through opposite holes from back to front. Trim ends at a slant. Glue rectangle on cover. Press letters and glue mouse on rectangle. With white gel pen, doodle three dots four times.

6 Arrange pieces on page. Glue down.

7 Add journaling on page with black marker.

YOU'RE A STAR!

Make a quick page using a background paper that is already printed with a checked border, cameras, and stars.

WHAT YOU NEED

12" x 12" Paper*:
- ❏ 1 camera border (background)
- ❏ 1 camera die-cut

8½" x 11" Paper:
- ❏ 1 yellow with white dots*
- ❏ 1 silver*

Cardstock:
- ❏ 1 black
- ❏ 1 yellow

- ❏ Yellow 1" letter stickers*
- ❏ Small star punch*
- ❏ Fine-tip black marker
- ❏ Small camera die cut* (optional)
- ❏ Adhesive
- ❏ Paper trimmer
- ❏ Pencil
- ❏ Ruler
- ❏ Scissors

*These products were used: Provo Craft® paper, letter stickers • Making Memories paper, die cuts • Canson paper • Marvy® Uchida punch

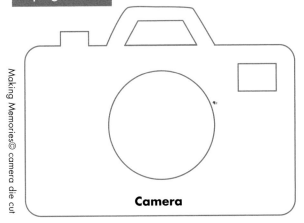

You're A Star
page 23

Camera

Making Memories© camera die cut

Say Cheese
page 22

Large Mouse Body

Small Mouse Body

WHAT YOU DO

Trace and cut out purple pattern on this page.

1 Punch out large camera and film-strip frame die cuts from paper. Cut two photos to fit inside die cuts. Glue photos on yellow paper. Cut around photos, leaving a thin border. Glue photos in center of die cuts. Glue camera on yellow paper. Cut around camera, leaving a thin border.

2 Trace and cut out camera pattern on this page from black paper. Glue small piece of yellow cardstock on back of camera so it shows through the circle. Punch four small yellow paper stars. Punch one silver star.

3 For journaling, cut a 2½" x 2¾" piece from silver paper. Glue on black cardstock. Cut around silver, leaving a thin border. Add journaling with black marker.

4 Arrange pieces on page. For title, press yellow letter stickers on background. Glue pieces down. With black marker, make small stitch lines around letters.

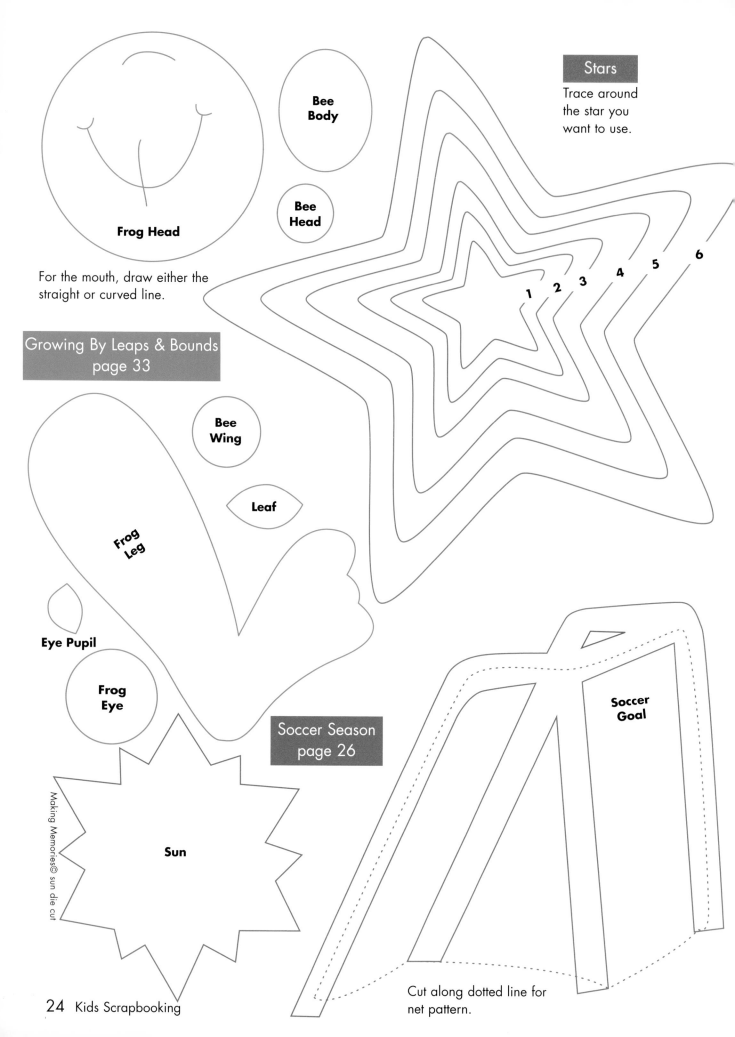

Frog Head

For the mouth, draw either the straight or curved line.

Bee Body

Bee Head

Growing By Leaps & Bounds
page 33

Bee Wing

Leaf

Frog Leg

Eye Pupil

Frog Eye

Sun

Making Memories© sun die cut

Stars

Trace around the star you want to use.

1 2 3 4 5 6

Soccer Season
page 26

Soccer Goal

Cut along dotted line for net pattern.

HAPPY BIRTHDAY STARS

*Cut your pictures into the shape of stars
and decorate the pages with stickers!*

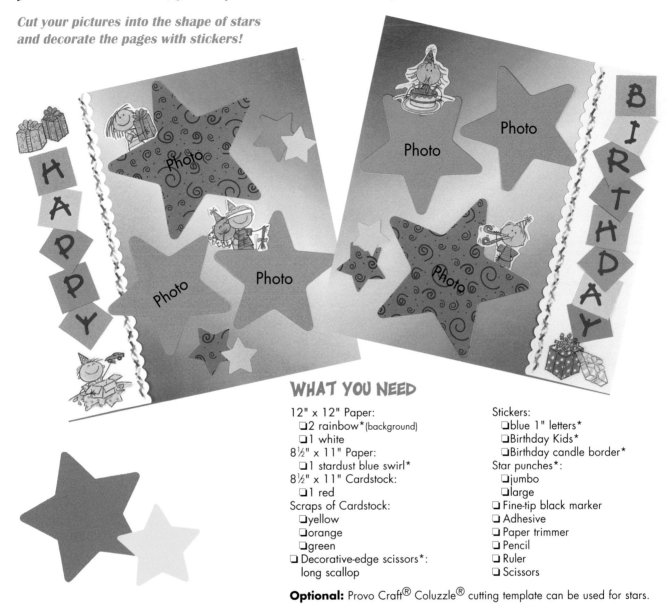

WHAT YOU NEED

12" x 12" Paper:
- ❏ 2 rainbow* (background)
- ❏ 1 white

8½" x 11" Paper:
- ❏ 1 stardust blue swirl*

8½" x 11" Cardstock:
- ❏ 1 red

Scraps of Cardstock:
- ❏ yellow
- ❏ orange
- ❏ green

❏ Decorative-edge scissors*:
  long scallop

Stickers:
- ❏ blue 1" letters*
- ❏ Birthday Kids*
- ❏ Birthday candle border*

Star punches*:
- ❏ jumbo
- ❏ large

❏ Fine-tip black marker
❏ Adhesive
❏ Paper trimmer
❏ Pencil
❏ Ruler
❏ Scissors

Optional: Provo Craft® Coluzzle® cutting template can be used for stars.

*These products were used: Amscan paper • Making Memories paper • Provo Craft® letter and border stickers • me & my BIG ideas™ stickers • Fiskars® scissors • Provo Craft® Coluzzle® border, knife, mat, paper • Marvy® Uchida punches

WHAT YOU DO

**Trace and cut out #4 and #6 stars
on the opposite page, or the size you want.**

1 For borders, cut two 4½" x 12" strips from white cardstock. With scallop-edge scissors, cut along one long edge of each strip. Press one candle border sticker along each scallop edge. Glue one border on outside edge of each rainbow background paper. Press birthday stickers on borders as shown.

2 For title, cut thirteen 1½" squares from scraps of cardstock. On left border, arrange five squares, overlapping and tilting them. Glue down. Press letter stickers on squares. On right border, arrange eight squares, overlapping and tilting them. Glue down. Press letter stickers on squares.

3 Use star patterns to trace around photos and cut out. Glue four photos on red and two photos on blue paper. Trim around photos, leaving a narrow border.

4 Punch out two jumbo stars from blue swirl paper and one from red cardstock. Punch out three large stars from yellow cardstock. Press four kid stickers on white cardstock. Cut around clear edge of stickers. Arrange pieces on pages. Glue down.

5 Add journaling with black marker.

SOCCER SEASON

Save your awards and team photo in the double pockets lined with soccer balls!

WHAT YOU NEED

12" x 12" Paper:
- ❏ 2 cloud* (background)

12" x 12" Cardstock:
- ❏ 2 green

8½" x 11" Cardstock:
- ❏ 1 white
- ❏ 1 black
- ❏ Blue 1" letter stickers*
- ❏ Soccer ball stickers*
- ❏ Boy paper doll kit*
- ❏ Sun die cut*
- ❏ White netting

Decorative-edge scissors*:
- ❏ grass
- ❏ cloud
- ❏ Double-stick tape (optional)
- ❏ Fine-tip black marker
- ❏ Adhesive
- ❏ Paper trimmer
- ❏ Pencil
- ❏ Ruler
- ❏ Scissors

*These products were used: Design Originals paper • Provo Craft® letter stickers, scissors • Frances Meyer, Inc® stickers • EK Success™ Paperkin® paper doll kit • Fiskars® scissors • Making Memories die cut

WHAT YOU DO

Trace and cut out blue patterns on page 24.

1 **Left page:** For pockets, use ruler and pencil to mark 10" up on one side of green cardstock. Measure 7" up on the other side of paper. Draw a line across page connecting the two marks. Cut on line, making two pocket pieces.

2 Lay the large pocket down with the 10" side on the left. Press soccer balls along the top edge so they just touch each other. Cut out around the top edge of stickers. Apply glue (or double-stick tape) close along the three uncut sides. Press pocket down on background with bottom edges even.

3 Lay the small pocket with the 7" side on the right. Press soccer balls along the top edge in the same way as large pocket and cut out around the top edge of stickers. Apply glue (or double-stick tape) close along the three uncut sides. Press pocket down over large pocket with the bottom edges even.

4 For title, press stickers across top of page. Press stickers on small pocket. Press several more soccer balls on page. Glue photo on black cardstock. Cut around photo with cloud-edge scissors. Place photo and memorabilia in pockets.

5 **Right Page:** For grass, cut one 2½" x 12" and one 5" x 12" strip from green cardstock. Cut top edges with grass-edge scissors. Glue narrow strip on top of wide strips with bottom straight edges even. Glue grass on background paper.

6 Trace and cut sun from yellow cardstock, soccer goal from white cardstock, and net from netting. Glue net behind goal.

7 For soccer player, glue paper doll pieces from kit together. *Option:* Use clothes in the kit to cut clothes from cardstock to match your team colors. Glue pieces together. Use stickers for numbers on the shirt. With black marker, draw neck, sleeve, and waist bands on shirt.

8 Glue photos on black cardstock. Cut around photos with cloud-edge scissors. Arrange pieces on page. Glue down. Press soccer ball sticker on grass.

9 Add journaling with black marker.

WET 'N WILD

Save summer memories in see-through vellum pockets! Add foam dots to the splashes so they pop off the page!

WHAT YOU NEED

12" x 12" Paper:
- ❏ 2 water* (background)
- ❏ 2 rock pathway*

12" x 12" Cardstock:
- ❏ 1 blue

8½" x 11" Paper:
- ❏ 1 blue vellum

8½" x 11" Cardstock:
- ❏ 1 yellow
- ❏ 1 red
- ❏ 1 orange
- ❏ 1 lime green

Paper dolls*:
- ❏ boy swimmer
- ❏ girl swimmer

- ❏ 2" Letter template

Splash punches:
- ❏ large
- ❏ small
- ❏ Foam dots
- ❏ Double-stick tape (optional)
- ❏ Fine-tip black marker
- ❏ Adhesive
- ❏ Paper trimmer
- ❏ Pencil
- ❏ Ruler
- ❏ Scissors

Optional: Provo Craft® Coluzzle® cutting template can be used for border.
C-Thru® Spunky template can be used for letters.

*These products were used: Amscan paper • Provo Craft® Coluzzle® border, knife, mat, paper • EK Success™ Paperkins® paper doll kits • C-Thru® Spunky letter template

WHAT YOU DO

Trace and cut out blue patterns on page 30.

1 For pockets, cut two 4¼" x 11" strips from blue vellum. Trace and cut out two 12" wavy borders from blue cardstock. Glue borders along top edge of each vellum strip. Apply glue (or double-stick tape) close along the bottom and outside edges. Press pocket down on background with bottom edges even. Do not put tape along the inner edges because it will show through the vellum. Just put a small piece of tape behind the border.

2 Cut rock paper to make a 1" to 1¼" wide frame for the top, bottom, and outside edges of the pages. Cut around shapes of rocks on inside of frame. Press foam dots on the back of frames every 3". Peel paper off dots and press frames on pages.

3 For paper dolls, glue pieces in each kit together. For title, trace and cut out letters from cardstock as shown. ***Option:*** *Carefully cut out the inside of the word "wet," leaving thin border.* Arrange on vellum pockets. Glue down.

4 Glue photos on different bright colors of cardstock. Cut around photos, leaving a thin border. Arrange pieces on pages. Tuck photos and paper dolls behind pockets. Glue down. Punch out three large and three small splash shapes. Use foam dots to attach splashes on pages.

5 Add journaling with black marker.

CUTE AS A BUG

Hide photos and journaling under the wings of the lady bugs.

WHAT YOU NEED

12" x 12" Paper:
- ❏ 2 grass*(background)
- ❏ 1 black with white dots*

12" x 12" Cardstock:
- ❏ 1 white
- ❏ 1 green

8½" x 11" Cardstock:
- ❏ 3 red
- ❏ 1 yellow
- ❏ 1 black
- ❏ 2" letter template*
- ❏ 4 brass fasteners
- ❏ 1 yard black-with-dots ribbon

Decorative-edge scissors*:
- ❏ cloud
- ❏ grass

Punches*:
- ❏ Circle - ¼", ¾"
- ❏ 2" Flower
- ❏ Small swirl
- ❏ Fine-tip black marker
- ❏ Adhesive
- ❏ Paper trimmer
- ❏ Pencil
- ❏ Ruler
- ❏ Scissors

Optional: Provo Craft® Coluzzle® cutting template can be used for circles.
Pebbles template can be used for letters.

*These products were used: Making Memories paper • Provo Craft® Coluzzle circle template, knife, mat, paper, scissors • Pebbles letter template • Fiskars® scissors • Marvy® Uchida punches

Open and close the wings to see the hidden photos.

WHAT YOU DO

Trace and cut out green patterns on page 29 and 30 and #6 circle on page 21.

1 For green title border, cut two 3½" x 12" strips from green cardstock. Cut long edges of strips with grass-edge scissors. Glue one strip ¼" up from the bottom of each page. Trace and cut two wavy borders from white cardstock. Glue the white strips on the green strips.

2 Trace and cut out letters from red cardstock. Glue letters on black cardstock. Cut around letters, leaving a thin border. Punch out five flowers from yellow cardstock. For flower centers, punch five ¾" circles from red cardstock. Glue centers on flowers. Arrange letters and three flowers on white border. Glue down. With black marker, doodle lines and dots on flowers and border.

3 Trace and cut eight bug wings from red cardstock. Use ¼" circle punch to make five or six holes in each wing Trace and cut eight bug wings slightly smaller than pattern from black dot paper. Glue red wings over black wings so black shows through the holes. Cut photos in circles to fit under the wings. Trace and cut four bug heads from black cardstock. For antenna, punch eight spirals from black cardstock.

4 Trace and cut out two large flowers from white cardstock, four large leaves from green cardstock, and four small leaves from green cardstock. Use pattern to cut two photos into circles. Glue the photos on red cardstock. Cut around photos, leaving a thin border. Glue photos on yellow cardstock. Cut around yellow border with cloud-edge scissors. Glue on large white flowers. Arrange pieces on the page. Glue down flowers, leaves, and lady bug heads.

5 Have an adult help you. Overlap ends of two wings. Poke paper fastener through both wings, head, and background paper. Spread open the prongs of the fastener on back of page. Repeat steps for each bug. Tie four ribbon bows. Cut ends at a slant. Glue bows on heads. Glue photos under the wings.

6 With black marker, doodle lines and dots on flowers and leaves. Add journaling.

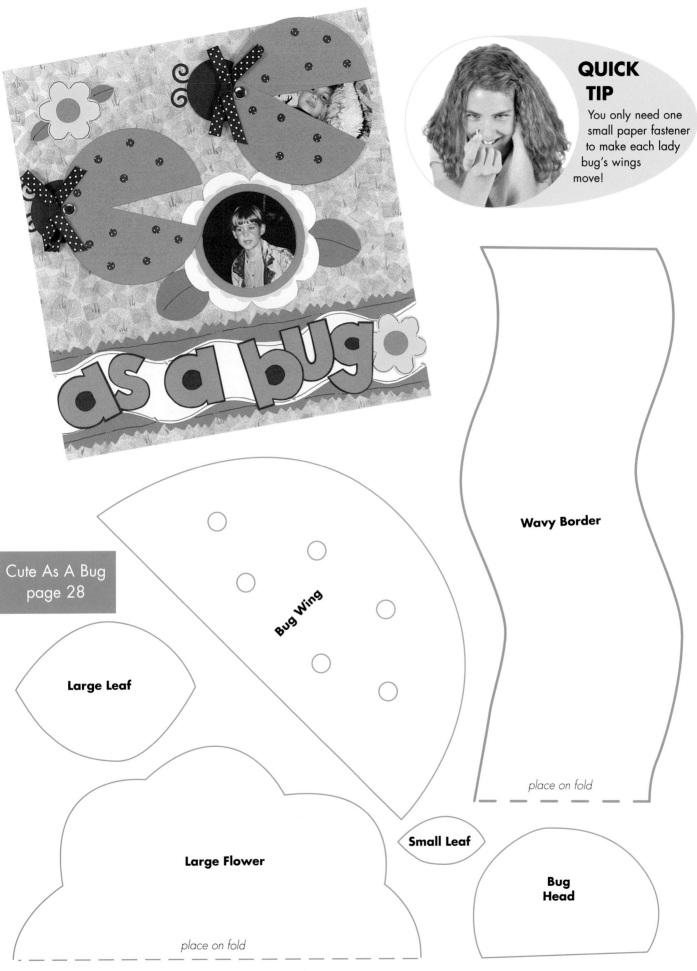

Cute As A Bug
page 28

QUICK TIP

You only need one small paper fastener to make each lady bug's wings move!

Wavy Border

place on fold

Bug Wing

Large Leaf

Small Leaf

Bug Head

Large Flower

place on fold

CUTE asbug

Pebbles© letter template

Cute As A Bug
page 28

WET·n WILD

C-Thru® Spunky letter template

Wavy Border

Wet 'n Wild
page 27

Provo Craft® Coluzzle® border template

MY FRIENDS

*Make a hearts & flowers page
for your friends' photos!*

WHAT YOU NEED

12" x 12" Paper:
- ❑ 2 yellow gingham (background)
- ❑ 1 raspberry gingham
- ❑ 1 blue gingham
- ❑ 1 yellow dot
- ❑ 1 raspberry dot
- ❑ 1 blue dot

12" x 12" Cardstock:
- ❑ 1 yellow
- ❑ 1 raspberry
- ❑ 1 blue
- ❑ Black 1" letter stickers*

- ❑ 3" letter template*
- Punches*(optional):
  - ❑ 3" Heart
  - ❑ 2¼" Daisy
  - ❑ 2¼" Flower
  - ❑ Circles - ¾", 1"
- ❑ Adhesive
- ❑ Paper trimmer
- ❑ Pencil
- ❑ Ruler
- ❑ Scissors

*These products were used: Making Memories paper • Provo Craft®
letter stickers • Marvy® Uchida punches • Family Treasures® punches
• C-Thru® Spunky letter template

WHAT YOU DO

**Trace and cut out #2 and #3 circles on page 21
and #5 heart on page 42.**

1 For left border, cut one 3¼" x 12" strip from yellow dot
paper. Glue on background paper. Cut one ¼" x 12" strip
from blue dot paper and glue next to the yellow strip. Trace
and cut (or punch) out eight hearts from different papers as
shown. Overlap and glue down on border. Press letter
stickers on the bottom heart.

2 For border across top of pages, trace and cut (or punch)
out seven hearts, four daisies, and three flowers from
different papers as shown. For the centers of the flowers,
trace and cut (or punch) out circles from different papers as
shown. Glue centers on flowers. Arrange the hearts and
flowers across the top of both pages.

3 For title, use a template to trace letters on blue dot paper.
Cut out letters. ***Option:*** *Use the ¾" circle punch to punch
out the center of the letters.* Place letters across the bottom
of both pages.

4 Cut seven ¼" x 6½" yellow strips. Place on pages,
connecting the hearts at the top to the letters at the bottom.

5 Glue photos on raspberry cardstock and cut around photos,
leaving a thin border. Repeat on yellow then blue
cardstock. Arrange pieces on page. Glue in place.

6 Add journaling with black marker.

DISNEYA

Provo Craft® Sizzix™ letter & paper doll die cuts

Body

Shirt

Shorts

Dress

Boy Hair #1

Boy Hair #2

Girl Hair

Boy Hair #3

Hair Bow

Bow Tie

Disney Days
page 37

Mouse Balloon

Accu-Cut® mouse balloon die cut

QUICK TIP

Draw lines for the bee "trails" with a pencil. Trace over lines with a black marker, making short dash lines. Wait a few minutes and erase pencil lines.

Add a dimensional foam dot behind each bee so they "pop" off the page.

GROWING BY LEAPS AND BOUNDS

Show how much you've changed through the years on a page full of punched circles!

WHAT YOU NEED

12" x 12" Cardstock:
- ❏ 2 turquoise (background)
- ❏ 1 yellow
- ❏ 1 white

8½" x 11" Cardstock:
- ❏ 2 lime green
- ❏ 1 yellow
- ❏ 1 bright pink
- ❏ 1 purple
- ❏ Scrap of black Cardstock
- ❏ Black 1" letter stickers*
- ❏ Acid-free decorative chalk*
- ❏ Foam dots

Punches* (optional):
- ❏ circle - ⅝", ¾", 1"
- ❏ square - 1⅜"

Decorative-edge scissors*:
- ❏ long scallop
- ❏ White gel pen
- ❏ Fine-tip black marker
- ❏ Adhesive
- ❏ Paper trimmer
- ❏ Pencil
- ❏ Ruler
- ❏ Scissors

Optional: Provo Craft® Coluzzle® cutting template can be used for circles.

*These products were used: Provo Craft® letter stickers, Coluzzle® circle template, knife, mat • Marvy® Uchida punches • Fiskars® scissors • Craf-T Products chalk

WHAT YOU DO

Trace and cut out green patterns on page 24 and #2 circle on page 21.

1. For title, cut two 1¾" x 12" strips from white cardstock. With black marker, doodle lines and dots along edges. Cut two 2½" x 12" strips from yellow cardstock. Center and glue white strips on yellow strips. Cut edges of yellow strip with long scallop-edge scissors.

2. Cut (or punch) out four 1⅜" squares from yellow cardstock. With black marker, doodle lines and dots around edges. Press capital letter stickers on squares. Arrange squares on title border and press small letter stickers in place between them, leaving room for the bee. Press one foam dot on back of each square. Peel paper off dot and press squares in place.

3. For frogs, trace and cut out four legs and two heads from lime green cardstock, four eyes from white cardstock, and four eye pupils from black cardstock. Glue frogs together as shown. With black marker, doodle lines and dots along the edges of each piece and draw a nose and mouth on each head. Use pink chalk to color cheeks. **Option:** *Draw eyeballs with black marker.*

4. For bees, trace and cut out three bodies from yellow cardstock, three heads from black cardstock, and six wings from white cardstock. Draw face with white gel pen. With black marker, outline body and wings. Glue bees together.

5. For flowers, trace and cut (or punch) out the following ¾" circles from cardstock: fifteen pink, fifteen purple, and six yellow. Trace and cut out eleven leaves from lime green cardstock. With black marker, outline each circle. Draw a line down center of each leaf.

6. Glue two photos on lime green cardstock. Cut around photos, leaving a wide border on bottom for journaling. Glue these photos and two other photos on yellow cardstock. Cut around photos, leaving a thin border. With black marker, doodle lines and dots around edges of frames.

7. Arrange pieces on pages. Glue down. With black marker, draw antennas on bees. Draw dash lines for bee "trails." Add journaling.

HAPPY BIRTHDAY

Use birthday stickers and tags to decorate a page filled with your party photos.

WHAT YOU NEED

The supplies to make the girl's pages are listed. Change the colors for the boy's page by looking at the picture.

12" x 12" Paper*:
- ❑ 2 yellow print (background)
- ❑ 1 green gingham
- ❑ 1 green dot
- ❑ 1 raspberry dot
- ❑ 1 blue dot
- ❑ 1 white with yellow dots
- ❑ Birthday sticker sheet*
- ❑ 6 large tags*

- ❑ 6 yellow ½" buttons
- ❑ Fine-tip black marker
- ❑ White glue
- ❑ Adhesive
- ❑ Paper trimmer
- ❑ Pencil
- ❑ Ruler
- ❑ Scissors

*These products were used: Provo Craft® paper • Making Memories paper • Stickopotamus® Stickerkin stickers • Paper Reflections tags

WHAT YOU DO

1 For borders, cut two 2¼" x 12" strips from green dot paper. Glue one border along the outside of each yellow print paper.

2 For left border, cut one ¼" x 12" strip from raspberry dot paper. Center and glue on green strip. For title, cut one 1¾" x 7½" strip from white dot paper. Place "Happy Birthday" sticker in center. With black marker, doodle lines, dots, and swirls around sticker. Center and glue white strip on green strip. Press balloon stickers above and below title. Draw string lines with black marker.

3 For right border, cut one 1¾" x 12" strip from white-with-yellow-dot paper. Place candle border sticker on band, ¼" from left side. Cut one ¼" x 12" strip from raspberry dot paper. Glue on right side of the border sticker. Center and glue white strip on green strip.

4 For background, cut two 6" x 7" pieces from green gingham paper. Place on pages.

5 For tags, cut two 3" x 5¼" pieces each from blue dot, green dot, and raspberry dot papers. Glue papers on tags. **Option:** *To make your own tag, cut a 3¼" x 6¼" piece from white cardstock. Cut two corners on one end at angles. Punch ¼" hole in center of tag between angled corners.*

With black marker, outline the top of each tag. Cut the legs off four paper doll stickers. Cut slits in arms. Tuck dolls into the tops of four tags and press in place.

6 Arrange pieces on pages. Glue down. Press additional stickers on tags and pages. Glue buttons on tags with white glue.

7 Cut photos to 2¾" x 5". Glue photos on tags.

8 Add journaling with black marker.

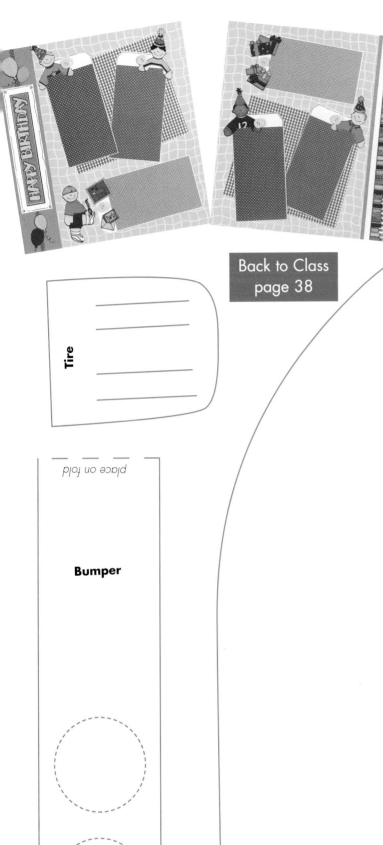

Change the characters and colors to make the page for a boy.

Taillight

Tire

Back to Class
page 38

place on fold

Bumper

School Bus

place on fold

FAITHFUL FRIENDS

Be sure to include your family pets in your album.
Attach a cute dog tag to your page!

WHAT YOU NEED

12" x 12" Paper:
- ❏ 2 paw print* (background)

12" x 12" Cardstock:
- ❏ 3 brown
- ❏ 3 red

8½" x 11" Cardstock
- ❏ 1 tan
- ❏ Red 1" letter stickers*
- ❏ Decorative-edge scissors: scallop
- ❏ Dog and cat stickers*

- ❏ Silver lanyard

Punches*:
- ❏ 2" Heart punch* (optional)
- ❏ ⅛" circle
- ❏ Fine-tip black marker
- ❏ Adhesive
- ❏ Paper trimmer
- ❏ Pencil
- ❏ Ruler
- ❏ Scissors

Optional: Provo Craft® Coluzzle® cutting template can be used for circles.

*These products were used: Design Originals paper • Provo Craft® Coluzzle® circle template, knife, mat, letter stickers • Mrs. Grossman's stickers • Fiskars® scissors • Marvy® Uchida punch

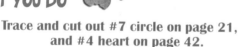

WHAT YOU DO

**Trace and cut out #7 circle on page 21,
and #4 heart on page 42.**

1 For background, cut two 10½" squares from paw print paper. Glue on red cardstock. Cut around square, leaving a thin border. Center and glue on brown cardstock.

2 For title, cut fifteen 1½" squares from tan cardstock. Glue each square on red cardstock. Cut around each square with scallop-edge scissors. Overlap eight squares on the left side of left page and seven squares on the right side of right page. Glue down. Press letter stickers on squares.

3 Trace circle on one photo and cut out. Glue photos on red cardstock. Cut around photo, leaving a thin border. Glue three photos on brown cardstock. Cut around photo, leaving a thin border.

4 Trace and cut (or punch) out heart from red cardstock. Print

on heart with black marker. Punch a ⅛" hole in heart and slip silver lanyard through the hole. Punch hole in circle frame. Slip lanyard through hole so the tag hangs down from photo. Glue photos on page.

5 Press dog and cat stickers on page.

6 Add journaling with black marker.

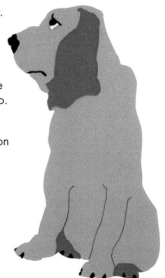

DISNEY DAYS

Dress the paper dolls to look like you and your family!

WHAT YOU NEED

12" x 12" Paper:
- ❏ 2 red stripe* (background)

12" x 12" Cardstock:
- ❏ 3 black

8½" x 11" Paper:
- ❏ 2 silver*
- ❏ 2 red vellum
- ❏ 1 shiny black
- ❏ 1 shiny red
- ❏ Mouse head punch

- ❏ Scraps of Paper & Cardstock for paper dolls
- ❏ Acid-free decorative chalk*
- ❏ Fine-point black permanent marker*
- ❏ Fine-tip black marker
- ❏ Adhesive
- ❏ Paper trimmer
- ❏ Pencil
- ❏ Ruler
- ❏ Scissors

Optional: Provo Craft® Sizzix Personal Die-Cut Machine can be used for letters and paper dolls.
Accu-Cut® Die-Cut Machine can be used for large mouse balloons.

*These products were used: Making Memories paper • Canson silver paper • Provo Craft® Sizzix die cuts • Accu-Cut® die cuts • Craf-T Products chalk • Sharpie marker

WHAT YOU DO

Trace and cut out purple patterns on page 32.

1 For background, cut two 8" x 9¾" pieces from red vellum. Center on silver paper and glue down IN THE CENTER ONLY. Cut around piece, leaving a ¼" border. Glue silver paper on black paper. Cut around, leaving ½" border. Glue black paper on red stripe paper.

2 For title, trace and cut out letters from black shiny paper. Punch 28 small mouse heads from black cardstock. Glue heads down sides of pages and one on each corner of the red vellum.

3 Glue photos on black cardstock. Cut around photos, leaving a thin border. Glue photos on silver paper. Cut around photo, leaving a ¼" border.

4 Trace and cut out paper dolls and clothes from colors of your choice. Glue pieces together.

5 Trace and cut out two bow ties from shiny red paper. Use permanent marker to outline the bow ties. Glue bow ties on black paper. Cut around bow ties, leaving a thin border. Trace and cut out three mouse balloons from shiny black paper.

6 Arrange pieces on pages. Tuck paper dolls behind photos. Glue down.

7 Add journaling with black marker.

BACK TO CLASS

Hop on the bus and save your back-to-school photos and facts in a little booklet!

WHAT YOU NEED

12" x 12" Paper:
- ❑ 1 school print* (background)

12" x 12" Cardstock:
- ❑ 1 yellow

8½" x 11" Paper:
- ❑ 1 silver*

8½" x 11" Cardstock:
- ❑ 1 yellow
- ❑ 1 white
- ❑ 1 green

Scraps of Cardstock:
- ❑ red
- ❑ black
- ❑ 2 apple stickers*

- ❑ Red letter stickers*: ½", 1"
- ❑ 9" of ⅞" red plaid ribbon*
- ❑ Circle punches*: ¼", 1"
- ❑ Decorative-edge scissors*: grass
- ❑ Grass die cut* (optional)
- ❑ White gel pen
- ❑ Fine-tip black marker
- ❑ Adhesive
- ❑ Paper trimmer
- ❑ Pencil
- ❑ Ruler
- ❑ Scissors

These products were used: Canson silver paper • Provo Craft® paper, letter stickers, scissors • Making Memories die cut • Frances Meyer, Inc® stickers • Offray ribbon

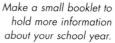

Make a small booklet to hold more information about your school year.

WHAT YOU DO

Trace and cut out red patterns on page 35.

1 Trace and cut out bus from yellow cardstock, bumper from silver paper, and two tires from black cardstock. Trace and cut (or punch) out four taillights from red cardstock. Glue bumper on bottom edge of bus. Glue taillights on bumper.

2 For sign, cut a small rectangle from white and print the name of your school on it with black marker. Glue on red cardstock. Cut around rectangle, leaving a thin border. Glue sign on bumper. With white gel pen, draw lines on tires. Arrange the pieces on background. Glue down.

3 To cut your photos, use the curve of the bus roof as a guide. The center photo should not be taller than 4½". Glue photos on the bus.

4 For booklet cover, cut one 3¾" x 6½" piece from yellow cardstock. For inside pages, cut one 3½" x 6¼" piece from white cardstock. Center and glue white piece on yellow cover. Fold in half to make the booklet. **Option:** Cut more

pieces for extra pages. Punch two ¼" holes along folded edge. Insert ribbon ends in holes from back to front. Tie a bow. Cut ends in a "v." Press small letter stickers for your name on the cover. Press on two apple stickers. Glue photos on pages inside the booklet. Print facts about the school year. Be sure to sign your name! Glue booklet on the school bus just below the center photo.

5 For title, press large red letter stickers on the bus on each side of the booklet.

6 For grass border, cut one 1" x 12" strip from green paper. Cut along one edge with grass-edge scissors. **Option:** Use a grass die cut. Glue grass along bottom edge of page.

Cut your own grass with a decorative-edge scissors.

MINI ALBUM

Decorate an album that is just the right size for class pictures of your friends.

WHAT YOU NEED

- ❏ 3" x 3" Mini Album
- Scraps of Cardstock:
  - ❏ red
  - ❏ black
  - ❏ your choice
- ❏ Photo corners
- ❏ School stickers
- ❏ Black fine-tip marker
- ❏ Adhesive
- ❏ Pencil
- ❏ Ruler
- ❏ Scissors

These products were used: Provo Craft® Mini album • Mrs Grossman's stickers • Fiskars® stickers

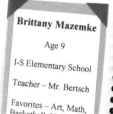 

3" x 3" Album

 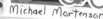

WHAT YOU DO

1 For the cover, use the computer or print the title on white paper. Cut a rectangle around the words. Glue rectangle on red paper. Trim around rectangle, leaving a thin border. Glue on black paper. Trim around rectangle, leaving a thin border. Glue title on album. Press school stickers on cover below title.

2 For inside front cover, use the computer or print information about your school year on 2" x 2½" piece of white paper. Glue on colored paper. Trim around rectangle, leaving a thin border. Place a photo corner on each corner. Moisten back of corners and press on inside cover.

3 For background papers, cut 2" x 2½" pieces from white paper. Glue class photos on colored paper. Trim around photos, leaving a thin border. Glue photos on white background paper. Print names under photos. Insert photos into plastic sleeves. Press stickers on plastic at edges of photos.

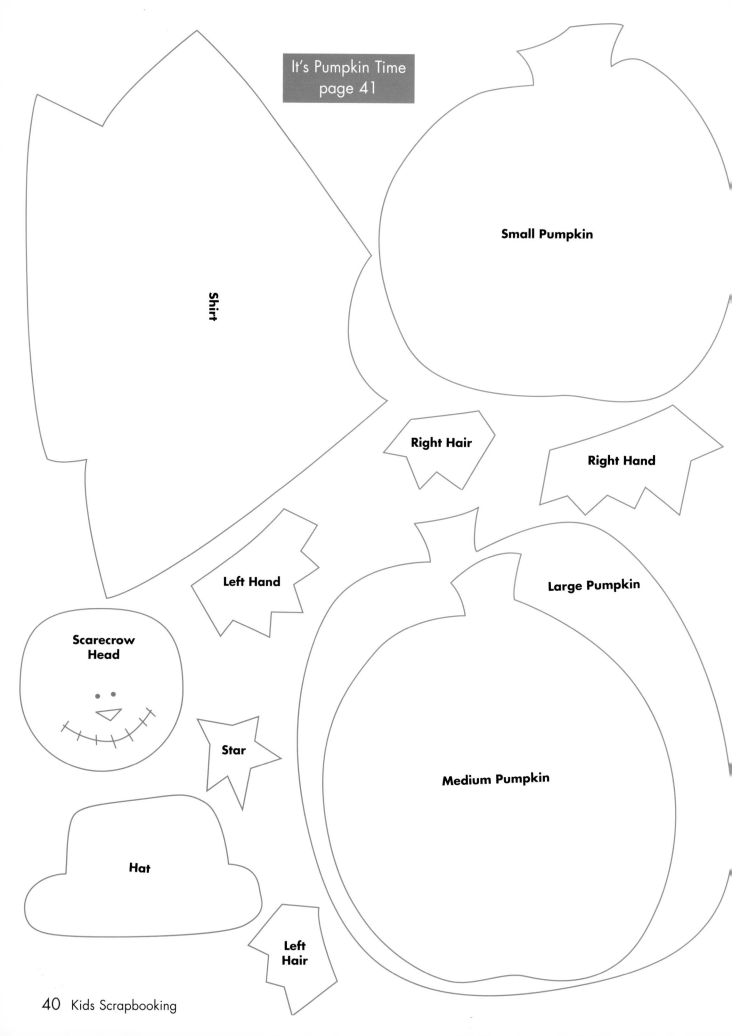

It's Pumpkin Time
page 41

Small Pumpkin

Shirt

Right Hair

Right Hand

Left Hand

Large Pumpkin

Scarecrow
Head

Star

Medium Pumpkin

Hat

Left
Hair

IT'S PUMPKIN TIME

Your fall pictures will be the pick of the patch on this paper-pieced pumpkin page!

WHAT YOU NEED

12"x 12" Paper:
- ❏2 denim dot* (background)
- ❏1 pastel yellow

8½" x 11" Paper:
- ❏1 apple for the teacher*

8½" x 11" Cardstock:
- ❏3 orange
- ❏1 red

Scraps of Cardstock:
- ❏light peach
- ❏brown
- ❏green
- ❏gold

❏ Black 1" letter stickers*

- ❏ Acid-free decorative chalk*
- ❏ Maple leaf punch*
- ❏ 8" of 1½" red gingham ribbon
- ❏ Foam dots
- ❏ Decorative-edge scissors*: dragonback
- ❏ Fine-tip black marker
- ❏ Adhesive
- ❏ Paper trimmer
- ❏ Pencil
- ❏ Ruler
- ❏ Scissors

*These products were used: Making Memories paper • Provo Craft® paper, letter stickers • Marvy® Uchida punch • Fiskars® scissors • Craf-T Products chalk

WHAT YOU DO

Trace and cut out green patterns on page 40.

1 Trace and cut out two large, two medium, and two small pumpkins from orange cardstock. Use red and orange chalk to add shading lines on the pumpkins. Use brown chalk to color the stems. Punch a green leaf for each pumpkin and cut off the stem. Glue leaves below pumpkin stems. With black marker, doodle curly lines on pumpkins.

2 For scarecrow, trace and cut out the following pieces from paper: hat from brown, hair and hands from yellow, head from light peach, shirt from apple print, star from gold. Arrange pieces on page, tucking the scarecrow behind three pumpkins. With black marker, draw face on the scarecrow. Color cheeks with red chalk. Doodle lines along edges of pieces. Tie ribbon in a bow and glue on the neck of scarecrow.

3 For title, cut fifteen 1" red squares and fifteen 1½" orange squares. Glue the orange squares in the center of the red squares. With black marker, doodle lines along edges of

red squares. Press letter stickers on each square. Place squares on pages across the top, slightly overlapping each other. Glue in place.

4 Glue photos on red cardstock. Cut around edge of red with decorative scissors. Glue three photos on orange cardstock. Cut around orange, leaving a thin border.

5 Arrange pieces on the pages. Glue down. Punch five leaves from green cardstock. Press foam dots on backs of leaves. Remove paper backing and press four leaves on title and one on a corner of one photo.

6 Add journaling with black marker.

Use red chalk to make the creases in the pumpkins.

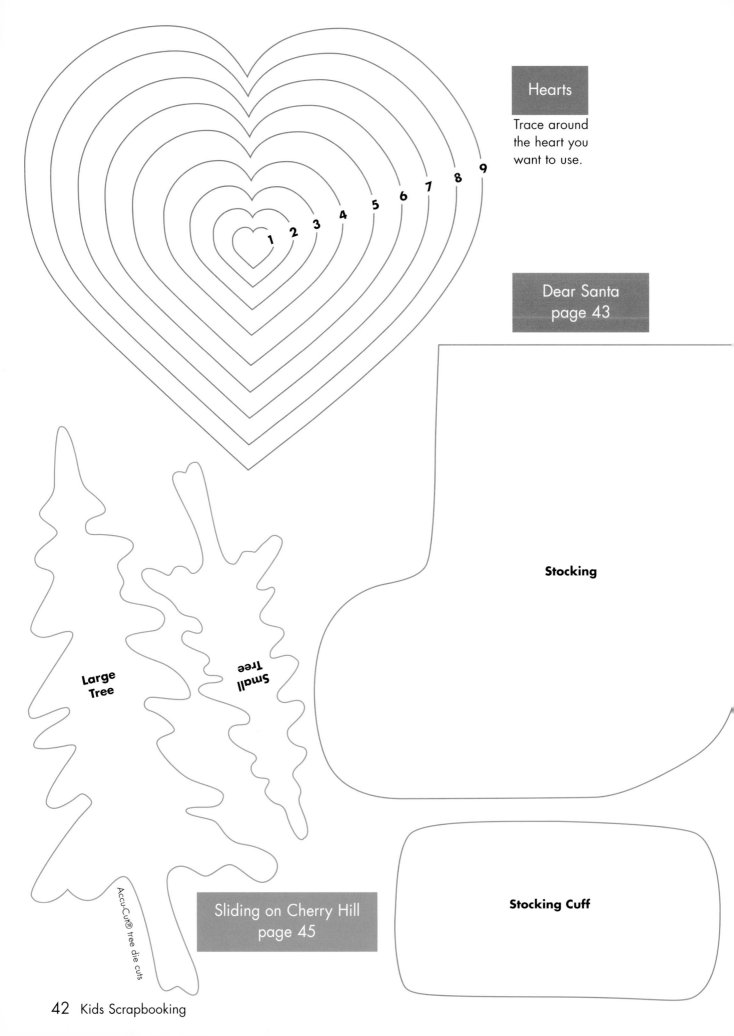

Hearts

Trace around
the heart you
want to use.

1 2 3 4 5 6 7 8 9

Dear Santa
page 43

Stocking

**Large
Tree**

**Small
Tree**

Accu-Cut® tree die cuts

Sliding on Cherry Hill
page 45

Stocking Cuff

DEAR SANTA

Decorate a page with Christmas paper and stickers to hold your holiday photos.

Make the stocking into a pocket to hold your Christmas list.

WHAT YOU NEED

12" x 12" Paper:
- ❏ 1 candy-cane print* (background)
- ❏ 1 red with green dot*

12" x 12" Cardstock:
- ❏ 1 white

8½" x 11" Cardstock:
- ❏ 1 green
- ❏ Christmas kids stickers*
- ❏ Christmas kids borders*
- ❏ Red ¾" letter stickers*
- ❏ Red ½" button

- ❏ Foam dots
- ❏ Decorative-edge scissors*: deckle
- ❏ Fine-tip black marker
- ❏ Double-stick tape (optional)
- ❏ White glue
- ❏ Adhesive
- ❏ Paper trimmer
- ❏ Pencil
- ❏ Ruler
- ❏ Scissors

*These products were used: Design Originals paper • Kangaroo and Joey paper • me & my BIG ideas™ stickers • Fiskars® scissors

WHAT YOU DO

Trace and cut out red patterns on page 42.

1 For border, cut a 3½" x 12" strip from red with green dot paper. Glue on left side of candy cane paper. Cut 3" x 12" strip from white cardstock. Center and glue on dot paper. Press border stickers down each side of white strip. Press Santa, tree, and letter stickers on white border.

2 Glue photos on green cardstock. Cut around photos, leaving a thin border. Glue on dot paper. Cut around photos, leaving a ¼" border.

3 Trace and cut stocking from green cardstock and cuff from white cardstock. Cut cuff edges with deckle-edge scissors. Attach foam dots on back of cuff. Remove paper backing and press cuff on top of stocking. With black marker,

doodle lines and dots along edges of stocking. Use white glue to attach button on top left corner of cuff. For Santa letter, cut a 2½" x 5" piece from white cardstock. Write a letter to Santa on it.

4 Arrange pieces on page. Glue photos in place. Apply glue close to edges along sides and bottom of stocking. Press on page. ***Option:*** *Cut pieces of double-stick tape in half lengthwise. Press tape along the edges on back of the stocking. Press stocking in place on page. Slide letter into stocking. Place two Christmas kids stickers on white cardstock. Cut around clear edge of the stickers and glue on page.*

5 Add journaling with black marker.

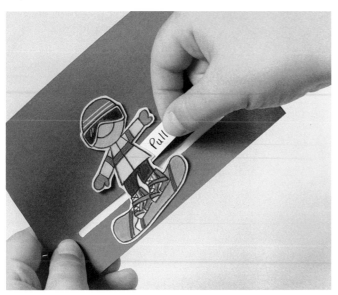

Pull a cutout shape across the page.

BASIC SLIDE

1 With a pencil, draw a light line on the background paper where you want the slide to go. With a scissor, cut a narrow slit in the background paper. Ask an adult to help you if you use a craft knife.

2 Cut slide pattern from cardstock. Fold to back along two inner fold lines. Fold to front along two outer fold lines.

3 Insert slide into slit in paper with folds in front and ends in back. Push slide back and forth in slit to make sure it slides smoothly.

4 Glue object on top of slide front.

5 If you want a pull tab, glue a ¼" x 2" strip of paper on back of object so it sticks out on one side. Print "pull" on the tab.

Cut a curvy line for more movement.

Slide Front

Slide Back

QUICK TIP

To use a sticker for an action object, press it onto white cardstock. Trim around sticker, leaving a narrow paper border.

Sliding on Cherry Hill
page 45

fold line	**Slide Platform**	fold line

SLIDING

Make a slide to add action to your page.

WHAT YOU NEED

12" x 12" Paper:
- ❏ 1 black plaid* (background)

12" x 12" Cardstock
- ❏ 1 red
- ❏ 1 white

8½" x 11" Cardstock:
- ❏ 1 speckled forest green*
- ❏ 1 forest green
- ❏ 1 blue
- ❏ 1 black
- ❏ Scrap of white Cardstock
- ❏ Red letter stickers*: ½", 1¼"
- ❏ Snowflake punch*
- ❏ Fine-tip black marker
- ❏ Adhesive
- ❏ Paper trimmer
- ❏ Pencil
- ❏ Ruler
- ❏ Scissors

Optional: Accu-Cut® die cuts can be used for trees.

*These products were used: Paperfever paper • Robin's Nest cardstock • Making Memories letter stickers • EK Success™ mini letter stickers • McGill punch • Accu-cut die cuts

Pull the sled up and down the hill.

WHAT YOU DO

Trace and cut out green patterns on page 42 & 44.

1 For background, cut one 11¾" square from black plaid paper. Center and glue on red cardstock.

2 For snow hills, tear cardstock in a variety of shapes. To tear paper, hold left side of the paper down on your work surface with left hand and pull the other side toward you with right hand.

3 Trace and cut four small pine trees from green cardstock and two from speckled green cardstock. Trace and cut one large pine tree from speckled green cardstock.

4 For photos, glue one photo on red and one on blue cardstock. Cut around photos, leaving a thin border. Silhouette the other photos. To silhouette a photo, carefully cut around the people, leaving a very thin border. Glue one of the photos on blue cardstock. Cut around the photo, leaving a thin border.

5 See page 44 to make the slide. Cut a slit in background through all layers. Insert slide. Glue sled photo on top of slide.

6 Arrange pieces on the page, tucking photos and trees behind snow banks. Glue in place. For title, press letter stickers slanted across the page. Press mini-letter stickers on the snow for the name of the hill. Punch three white snowflakes. Glue on page.

7 Add journaling with black marker.

GLOSSARY

What Does It Mean?

Acid free: products that have no acid in them or an object that has a Ph of 7.0 or more

Adhere: when two things stick to each other

Adhesive: a substance that makes one object stick to another one

Asymmetrical: when two things look balanced but do not look exactly alike

Cardstock: paper that comes in three weights – lightweight, medium-weight, and heavy-weight; medium-weight is most often used in scrapbooking

Corner punch: used to trim corners of paper into decorative shapes

Crop: cutting a photo to remove the unwanted background

Craft knife: a knife with a replaceable blade used to cut straight edges and small spaces

Cutting mat: a protective rubber mat used when cutting with a craft knife

Cutting template an acrylic pattern that has channels to guide a craft knife in cutting out a shape

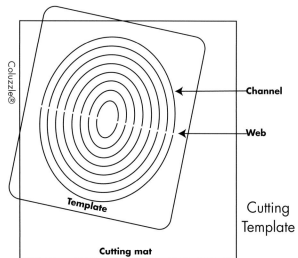

Coluzzle®

Channel

Web

Template

Cutting mat

Cutting Template

Decorative-edged scissors: paper scissors that have a pattern along the blade edges

Die: the template blade used to cut out a shape when it is pressed down using a die-cutting machine

Die cut: the cutout shape that is made using a die-cutting machine

Glue stick: a fairly dry glue that works well on photos and paper

Journal: to give the facts or details behind the photos and memorabilia

Laminate: to protect an object by placing it between two sheets of plastic

Light box: a box with an acrylic (or glass) top that has a light inside it; used for tracing and to see through thin materials

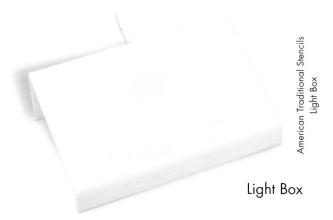

American Traditional Stencils
Light Box

Light Box

Mat: a frame that creates a border around a photo

Memorabilia: items that are saved from events that have special meaning

Mount: to adhere a photo onto paper

Mounting tape: has adhesive on both sides

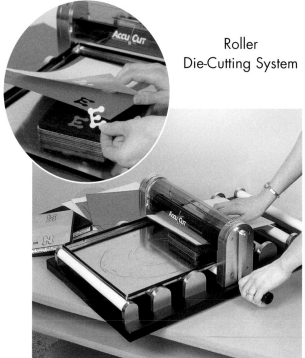

Roller
Die-Cutting System

Accu-Cut® Die-Cutting System

Fiskars® Paper Trimmer

Paper Crimper

aper crimper: a paper press that makes textured folds in paper when paper passes through its rollers; the paper looks corrugated

age protector: a plastic envelope that fits over an album page

aper trimmer: a tool that cuts paper by sliding a blade along a straight channel

h testing pen: used to tell the amount of acid in paper by seeing how the ink changes color

hoto corner: small triangle pockets with adhesive on the back that fit over the corners of photos to hold them in place on a page

hoto sticker square: a small square that has adhesive on both sides; used to adhere photos (or other items) on paper

ed-eye pen: a pen with dye that filters out the red in eyes in photos

tencil: a pattern used for tracing a shape

wivel craft knife: a knife with a replaceable blade used to cut straight and curved edges; works well when using a template as a guide

ymmetrical: when two things that look exactly alike have balance

emplate: patterns that can be used many times; clear acrylic ones are easy to position accurately

Vellum: paper that is semi-transparent so you can see through it

Press
Die-Cutting System

Sizzix® Die-Cutting System

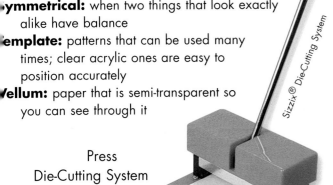

SOURCES

Accu-Cut® Systems
(800) 288-1670
www.accucut.com

All Night Media®, Inc.
(800) STAMPED
www.plaidonline.com

Amscan, Inc.
(914) 345-3884
www.amscan.com

The C-Thru® Ruler Company
(800) 243-8419
www.cthruruler.com

Canford
(800) 278-1783
www.daler-rowney.com

Cock-A-Doodle Design™
(800) 262-9727
www.cockadoodledesign.com

Colors by Design
(800) 832-8436
www.colorsbydesign.com

Craft-T Products
(507) 235-3996
www.craf-tproducts.com

Design Originals
(800) 877-7820
www.d-originals.com

DMD® Industries, Inc.
(800) 805-9890
www.dmdind.com

Dress It Up™
www.JesseJamesButton.com

EK Success™
(800) 524-1349
www.eksuccess.com

Ellison®, Inc
(800) 253-2238
www.ellison.com

Family Treasures®, Inc
(800) 413-2645
www.familytreasures.com

Fiskars®
(715) 842-2091
www.fiskars.com

Frances Meyer, Inc®
(800) 372-6237
www.francesmeyer.com

Hot Off The Press
(503) 266-9102
www.hotp.com

K & Company
(888) 244-2083
www.kandcompany.com

Kangaroo & Joey
(800) 646-8065
www.kangarooandjoey.com

The McCall Pattern Co.
www.wallies.com

McGill, Inc.
www.mcgillinc.com

Making Memories
(801) 294-0430
www.makingmemories.com

Marvy® Uchida
www.uchida.com

me & my BIG ideas™
(949) 589-4607
www.meandmybigideas.com

Mrs. Grossman's Stickers
(800) 429-4549
www.mrsgrossmans.com

My Mind's Eye™, Inc.
(800) 665-5116

Offray
www.offray.com

Paperfever
(801) 412-0495
www.paperfever.com

Pebbles in My Pocket®
(800) 438-8153
www.pebblesinmypocket.com

Provo Craft®
(800) 937-7686
www.provocraft.com

ScrapEase
www.whatsnewltd.com

Sonburn, Inc.
(925) 239-2888

The Stamping Station
(801) 444-3828
www.stampingstation.com

Stickopotamus®
(888) 270-4443
www.stickopotamus.com

EVEN MORE FUN FOR KIDS...AND ADULTS!

More Than Memories

The Complete Guide For Preserving Your Family History

edited by Julie Stephani

Includes hundreds of tips and techniques to instruct and inspire you to create beautiful family albums that will be cherished for generations to come! Clear step-by-step instructions show you how to organize, protect, and display your treasured photos.

Softcover • 8½x11 • 128 pages 225 color photos

Item# MTM • $14.95

More Than Memories II

Beyond the Basics

edited by Julie Stephani

The second book in the series goes beyond the basics to include step-by-step instructions on photo tinting, paper embossing, and photo transferring, as well as ideas on making greeting cards, puzzles, and time capsules. Includes 13 themed page layout ideas, including Heritage, Home and Family, Babies, Vacations, Weddings, and much more.

Softcover • 8¼x10⅞ • 128 pages 200 color photos

Item# MTMB • $16.95

More Than Memories III

Mastering the Techniques

edited by Julie Stephani

Each chapter focuses on a technique and uses projects to illustrate the tips and tricks for mastering the specific tools, products and applications. Learn new and better ways for creative cropping, journaling, rubber stamping, organizing and paper piecing to help you create wonderful keepsake books.

Softcover • 8¼x10⅞ • 128 pages 120 color photos

Item# MTM3 • $16.95

Ultimate Scrapbook Guide

by Julie Stephani

The fourth book in the best-selling More than Memories series is here! Master-scrapbooker Julie Stephani answers the most often asked questions about scrapbooking. Included are hundreds of creative scrapbooking ideas and projects, expert tips and advice on a wide variety of techniques.

Softcover • 8¼x10⅞• 128 pages Color throughout

Item# MTM4 • $19.95

Shape Your Memories

Creating One-of-a-Kind Scrapbook Pages

by Patti Swoboda

Add new dimension to your scrapbook pages! You'll learn how to use common scrapbooking tools and Staedtler's Hot Foil Pen to create shaped pages and page protectors. Features 12 projects and variations, including a bell that can be transformed into a frog, penguin, elephant, monkey, and even a dog!

Softcover • 8¼x10⅞ • 48 pages 75 color photos & more than 50 full-size patterns

Item# SYM • $10.95

Kids 1st Summer Crafts

by Krause Publications

How many times have you heard "I'm bored" from your children during the summer? No more! In this booklet kids ages 5 to 13 will find hours of enjoyment from 20 different crafts, games and activities, designed especially for them. With easy-to-follow instructions and projects suitable for all skill levels, this idea book will keep your kids going all summer long!

Softcover • 8¼x10⅞ • 24 pages 25 color photos

Item# K1SC • $6.95

Kids 1st Christmas Crafts

by Krause Publications

Kids ages 5 to 13 will love making-and giving-any of the 20 projects in this holiday collection. Projects made with such materials as wire, polymer clay, Styrofoam, and felt, include ornaments, centerpieces, garland, a snow globe, and a scrapbook page, each with step-by-step instructions.

Softcover • 8¼x10⅞ • 32 pages Color throughout

Item# K1XMAS • $6.95

Got Tape?

Roll Out the Fun With Duct Tape!

by Ellie Schiedermayer

Picture frames, purses and postcards made from duct tape? That's right! Now you can learn more than 25 fun, kooky, and unique new ways to utilize everyone's favorite fix-all. Each project includes easy-to-follow instructions and step-by-step photographs and requires no more than duct tape, scissors, and optional embellishments.

Softcover • 8¼x10⅞ • 48 pages 50 color photos

Item# DUCT • $7.95